Inspiring Mental Toughness Workbook for Junior Sports Stars

Build Unshakeable Resilience, Enhance Focus and Increase Confidence in Just 30 Days With 50+ Mental Toughness Drills and Exercises

Chest Dugger

Table of Contents

Table of Contents 2
About the Author 3
Disclaimer 4
Introduction: Why Mental Grit is Your Secret Weapon in Sports. 5
Eight Slam-Dunk Traits of Mental Toughness 7
How Muhammad Ali Shrugging Off Life's Punches 14
Lou Gehrig's Trick to Ignoring the Noise and Nailing the Play.. 34
Niki Lauda's Masterclass in Ditching Instant Wins 51
Tiger Woods' Blueprint for Believing You're the Boss 59
John McEnroe's Art of Thinking Fast and Flipping the Script ... 70
Fire in the Gut: Simone Biles' Deep-Down Drive to Crush It 88
Jesse Owens' Positivity Hack to Leap Over Life's Hurdles 100
Eric Dier's Guide for Keeping Your Head 114
30 Days to a Titanium Mind: Mental Toughness Bootcamp 128

About the Author

Chest Dugger is a soccer fan, a former professional and coach. He is fascinated by the mental side of sport, as well as the physical. Enjoy this book and several others that he has written.

Disclaimer

Copyright © 2025

All Rights Reserved

No part of these works can be transmitted or reproduced in any form including print, electronic, photocopying, scanning, mechanical, or recording without prior written permission from the author.

Introduction: Why Mental Grit is Your Secret Weapon in Sports

There are many elements to sporting success. But perhaps two are more significant than the rest. The first is our physical make up, something determined by many factors. Genetics, training, diet, facilities and equipment to enhance training to name but a few. But we also need mental strength to succeed as an athlete. In fact, many would argue that it is this element that separates the truly elite from the very good.

This book will illustrate aspects of mental toughness through the stories of some of the most powerful performers in history. It will also offer a comprehensive list of drills which can be used to enhance our mental fortitude.

Of course, there are many secondary benefits to developing our mental strength. Our confidence will grow, we will recover more quickly from setbacks, we will be happier, and our self-esteem will improve. Not just in the sporting sense, either, but in our everyday lives.

There is much evidence out there on the physical benefits of sport to our well-being, but the same is true for our emotional and mental health. Sport is the fun activity which keeps on giving, and this book seeks to help us make the most of what it can offer, whilst at the same time improving our own performance within it.

Eight Slam-Dunk Traits of Mental Toughness

We are now going to consider some of the greatest sportsmen and women in history. The thing about the most elite of sports players is that they combine incredible physical prowess – strength, skill, technique – with overwhelming mental strength. They possess all of the aspects of mental toughness discussed in this chapter in abundance. The following chapters each focus on one athlete, and one type of mental strength which has enabled that champion to reach and remain at the top of their game. That we focus on the athlete and one of these strengths does not in any way imply that they do not possess all of the other aspects of mental acuity which are needed to be the best that you can be.

Nor does it imply that there are no other athletes who possess this strength at equal, perhaps even greater (if that is possible) levels. To be a great athlete requires that you push yourself through not only physical barriers, but mental ones too.

So, what are these eight traits of great mental strength which are possessed by the finest athletes? They are (not in any order of importance):

1. Resilience
2. Focus
3. Self-Discipline
4. Confidence
5. Mental Flexibility
6. Intrinsic Motivation
7. Optimism
8. Emotional Regulation

Let us spend a moment understanding why each of these traits is so important. **Resilience** is the ability to rebound from setbacks. It is the nature of sports that we suffer setbacks from time to time. Such setbacks can vary in intensity. We might find losing a vital match or event difficult when we expect to do better. We may find ourselves dropped by the team. We might make a crucial error, perhaps one which costs us the result we desire. We may receive criticism from our teammates, coaches or even supporters. We might simply have a bad game. If our resilience is strong, then not only do we quickly recover from our disappointment, but we find within ourselves the ability to take that disappointment and use it to help us improve our own performance.

Focus is crucial in top sports players. It is rare indeed that our opponents are sufficiently less talented than ourselves that we do not need to be at our best, or close to it, to perform as we would wish. And even if we sometimes win with poor focus, then our own sense of satisfaction is diminished if we know we have not maintained concentration. More than that, it is the nature of sport that it so often rests on crucial moments and actions. A defensive player losing the player they are meant to be marking can cost a game, losing track of a fellow racer can mean they shoot past whilst we find ourselves trapped in the pack. Focus requires not only strong concentration, but that intensity of mind must be maintained throughout both the match, and the training which prepares us for the match.

Self-discipline is another trait which must stay with us both in competition and out of it. It takes many forms. These include the self-discipline to train and prepare properly; the importance of maintaining physical and verbal discipline, even when provoked, the vital role played of looking after ourselves – getting enough sleep and the right nutrition. It is also a part of self-discipline that we know when to stop, when to relax, when to take a break. The best athletes do not take a break from their regime, they build appropriate breaks into it.

Confidence is another key aspect of mental strength. Athletes take risks; they are calculated risks but risks, nonetheless. The best athletes see their risks succeed more often, but they also have the confidence in themselves to accept that sometimes they will fail, and they know that when they do, that is fine. The soccer player who shoots rather than plays the safe pass, the runner who holds off their sprint finish until the right time, the quarterback who spies the space and backs themselves to find it, the tennis player who goes for the winner rather than prolonging the rally. These are the sports players who win games.

Mental flexibility is linked to confidence. Sport requires thinking on your feet, knowing when to apply your strategy and when to adapt it to the circumstances of the moment. Sports players who have the mental flexibility to adapt to the circumstances of the event, once more, are those who succeed the most.

Intrinsic Motivation. Sport is great fun. Who would not want to become a pro in the sport they love? But it is hard work. It requires great motivation. Imagine swimmers getting up at 5.00 am on a cold wet morning to train when the pool is free from casual length-trawlers. The athlete pushes themselves in pre-season, suffering pain, nausea, stiffness. To some extent, those around us – teammates, fellow athletes, coaches, our loved ones – can provide some of that motivation, but ultimately we need to want it ourselves. We do so even when it hurts, or we'd rather be doing something else. In fact, when scouts and coaches are looking for potential, intrinsic motivation is one of the key traits they seek. Yes, they want athleticism appropriate to the sport, technique and a strong skillset, but beyond that, they need to see in their prospects the desire to succeed.

Optimism is one of the most important traits. There is a theory which carries much weight among life coaches and those who work in mental health. It argues that those with a positive outlook succeed more than those with a negative one. Such people find they attract other positive folk to them, offering mutual support and growth. They become excellent leaders and role models; they see opportunities even in their rare failures.

Emotional Regulation focusses on our ability to control our emotions. Sport is emotional by its very nature. It is also tiring, and most of us find our emotions swirl more violently when we are tired. Athletes with good emotional regulation can control their emotions, can stay calm under pressure. This means, simply, that they make better decisions, and good decisions lead to good outcomes.

We will begin to look at some of the greatest athletes in history by considering perhaps the greatest, certainly by his own definition, of all time. Somebody who possessed all of the above traits in abundance.

The inestimable, remarkable, so much loved, and so sadly missed, Muhammad Ali.

Reward 1:

As a bonus, we'd like to offer a printable version pdf of all the visual drills in this workbook.

The printable version of this book contains 1 or 2 fill in drills.

The below pdf helps you focus on certain drills. If there's a certain drill that you want to perform everyday you can download the pdf and print out as many copies of that particular drills as you need.

Just scan the QR code below to access the pdf.

Bounce-Back Ability: How Muhammad Ali Shrugging Off Life's Punches

Resilience – The Ability to Recover Quickly From Setbacks

It goes without saying that Muhammad Ali could exemplify every single one of the categories of mental strength we cover in this book. What could require more focus than fighting the strongest men on the planet, when one blow from their mighty fist might not only end your career, but also your life? What can require greater self-discipline than honing your massive frame into the strongest, fittest shape it can be? What requires more emotional regulation than knowing you must survive another three, six, nine minutes, when completely exhausted, in order to achieve your dream? Minutes during which your opponent has nothing to lose, and is trying to destroy you? Muhammad Ali's confidence, as well, is of course legendary. He too possessed both that intrinsic motivation and positive mindset to achieve his goal, to become the most famous athlete on the planet, all against seemingly impossible odds. However, it not only seems appropriate to begin our brief journey with 'The Greatest', but to use his story to illustrate the importance of resilience. Because overcoming injury, or your opponent, or physical or emotional problems requires incredible resilience, but when success means overcoming racial prejudice from your own nation, the level of resilience needed enters a whole new level.

Because Muhammed Ali faced every setback it could be possible to face, including the ones that should never appear in any sport, or any aspect of life, indeed. Racism and religious persecution. Unable to hurt him, to belittle him, to destroy him in any other way, those in power in the US at the time decided they would attack him on the basis of his ethnicity and his religious beliefs. Did they destroy him? It would take more than people like that to destroy 'the greatest'!

Cassius Marcellus Clay Jr was born in Louisville, Kentucky on January 17th, 1942, He is the older of Cassius Marcello Sr and Odessa Grady Clay's two sons. He is introduced to boxing at the age of 12. Young Cassius's bike is stolen, and he reports the theft to a local policeman and pillar of the community, Joe Martin. Joe also happens to coach boxing at the local youth center, as well as hosting a local TV show called 'Tomorrow's Champions.' Cassius demonstrates natural grace, movement and technique, and it is not long before the young lad is appearing on his mentor's TV show.

Under the guidance of Fred Stoner, an African American boxing trainer, Cassius quickly advances. It is his movement that catches the eye, meaning he can dodge and weave and rarely get hit. Then, such grace is not completely surprising, even for a boy who is clearly going to turn into a very large man. His father might be a sign painter by trade, but he is also a keen amateur entertainer, who loves to sing, dance and act. Performance, we might conclude, is in Cassius's blood.

Tournaments fall to the powerful, big hitting but light on his feet boxer. Then, aged just 18, he wins gold in the light heavyweight division at the Rome Olympics. It is shortly after this period that he wins a huge contract with a group of rich local sponsors. Things really are on the up for the young boxer. Of course, he is a media dream, with catch phrases attached to him and nicknames applied. His movement combined with powerful hitting means he can 'float like a butterfly, and sting like a bee.' Later, his penchant for composing poems, usually about his boxing talents, lead him to acquire the nickname 'The Louisville Lip.'

It is no surprise that, aged just twenty-two (a fledgling in heavyweight boxing terms) he defeats the mighty Sonny Liston to become world champion.

But despite the success, Cassius is a black man during a time of great political and social prejudice in the USA. Inspired by Malcolm X, he is attracted to the Black Muslim Faith, a group that not only promotes Islam but also a separate black nation in America. Cassius changes his name to Cassius X and later is given the name Muhammad Ali.

It is in 1966 that he is known to have come to the attention of the FBI. Ali is already widely acclaimed to be the greatest boxer who has ever lived. He punches so quickly and with such power that often the strikes he delivers are not even seen by his audience. Famously, in his first title defense, a rematch against Liston, he delivers a blow so fast that it becomes known as the 'phantom punch.' He is also a showman, a significant role model for African Americans and politically of a persuasion unpopular with the white establishment. It is perhaps then hardly surprising that, rare among leading sportsmen of the time, Ali just happens to be conscripted to fight in the Vietnam war. As Jack Hunter writes, in his excellent article for the Austin American-Statesman in the summer of 2016 (marking Muhammad Ali's death following the debilitating Parkinson's Disease which impacted his later life) Ali was not a draft dodger. Firstly, he correctly argues that as a religious preacher he is excused the draft. (Before his return to the ring in 1970 the Supreme Court confirms the validity of this argument.) Secondly, he does not dodge the draft, instead he refuses to participate in a war with which he does not agree. He attends his call up appointment but refuses to step forward to be conscripted. He is aware that in doing so the American State will imprison him, end his career, cost him his fortune and ruin his life. These are consequences he is prepared to face. He is sentenced to five years in prison, although the sentence is waived. But he is banned from the ring.

Ali is in his late twenties by the time he is allowed to return to the ring. His title has gone to Joe Frazier, another Olympic gold medalist. Ali realizes that his years away from the ring, combined with the slowing impact of age, means he needs to reinvent himself. This was brought home when Frazier defeated him a few months after his return to boxing. So, not only must he recover from the setbacks of having his career curtailed by political motivations, his reputation destroyed by the right-wing establishment in the media and the halls of power but also from the awareness that boxing has moved on, whilst he, in fighting terms, has not. How could he, away from the sport he loves, mount a comeback?

Ali develops the tactic he calls 'rope a dope'. Basically, this involves covering up on the ropes whilst his opponent burns himself out, before bursting powerfully out with devastating blows of his own. It is a style exemplified when Ali regains his world title defeating the fearsome George Foreman in the 'rumble in the jungle' in 1974. Here, the mighty Foreman, a ferocious hitter, pummels Ali for seven rounds. It seems that the former champion must succumb. Then, out of the blue in the eighth round, Ali explodes from the ropes with a combination of strikes which send Foreman crashing to the deck, knocked out.

It is worth noting that a man as resilient as Ali not only defeats the might of the American establishment and his opponents in the golden age of heavyweight boxing. He becomes a highly respected statesman too. He supports Jimmy Carter in his successful 1974 campaign for the

White House and is active in supporting causes addressing poverty and the plight of children. He becomes, probably, the most loved and admired sportsman in the history of sport. He not only demonstrates that crucial mental strength to come back quickly from setbacks – even when that setback is caused by the might of the American state – but truly deserves the accolade of being 'The Greatest.' We hear so much about the 'goat' these days. In truth, there is only one.

Mental Toughness Drills To Develop Resilience

While we may struggle to get to Mohammad Ali's level of resilience, let's have a look at a few Mental Toughness drills that can help us grow our own resilience.

Drill 1: Visualize Historic Comebacks

Think about Mohammad Ali. Think about Novak Djokovic. Think about your favorite sports team. What's your favorite moment about them? It's likely their biggest comeback. This exercise is meant to put you in the shoes of your successful heroes and write down the actions that they took that made them successful. For each of these situations, you're going to imagine you're the main character. You're going to describe the imaginary situation, the actions you took when the situation happened, the results, and the feeling after you achieved the goal.

This can help you visualize success in tough situations.

Situation 1 (where your player/team is in trouble):

Describe how you felt:

Actions You Took:

Results:

Drill 2: How To Reverse Losses

Now, let's look at another situation where your favorite team loses a close game. Put yourself in that situation and visualize how you could have done something differently and reverse the situation. You can write in the space below or in your notebook your visualized success.

Situation 1 (where your team lost):

Your Feelings As the Main Player:

Actions You Took that Might Have Led to A Different Outcome:

Positive Results of Actions:

Drill 3: Have a Realistic Measure for Success

In any two-team sport, half the competitors are going to lose. In a league, only one team will win. In a large cycling race, far more competitors lose than win. Every one of our competitors seeks victory. Most, by definition, will fail. Therefore, we must set realistic targets to measure our success.

The Drill: These reasonable targets could include setting a PB (Personal Best); improving our position from our last event; following our strategy; feeling we have done our best. Relating back to the importance in trusting our strategy, if our only measure of success is becoming the overall winner, we will fail more often than we succeed, especially as we improve through the levels of competition. Thus, we will never develop the trust we need in our strategy, which is essential if we are to fulfil our potential. But a realistic measure of success improves our opportunity to trust in ourselves. You can document your performances over time in a table similar to the one below. Also make sure you have a realistic goal recorded before each session.

Success comes…when we are able to rate our measure of success higher than winning or losing.

DATE	GOAL TODAY	PERFORMANCE TODAY	PERSONAL BEST

Drill 4: Rehearsal

We have touched on this already. **Visualizing** an action helps to make it more likely to succeed.

The Drill: Here we rehearse a much larger play. For example, our strategy for running a race. For a fast finisher it might look like this. Our example uses an 800m track race.

Rehearsed Strategy One: Stay within touch of the leading group on the first lap.

Rehearsed Strategy Two: Move wide into space on the final back straight.

Rehearsed Strategy Three: Stay in the top three off the final bend.

Rehearsed Strategy Four: Sprint full out for the last thirty meters.

Success comes…when we can enact the strategy we visualize.

Drill 5: Best Practice

Forgive the pun, but if we practice, or (in the sporting sense) train, with maximum effort we are really employing best practice. For most athletes, training is sometimes a chore and usually of secondary pleasure to competition.

The Drill: Note your mood going into training and use all the positive reinforcement techniques you have acquired to get your mind into maximum focus and its most positive state.

Success comes…when you only rarely need to use this technique!

Drill 6: Mantra – Be Positive (1)

A *positive* mantra builds our self-esteem, which is essential to dealing with hard situations on the field. Fighting back from tough situations is the essence of resilience.

The Drill: Write five positive mantras about yourself, at least three relating to your sporting activity. For example: 'I am strong…' and 'I am resilient.' Say them in your head, or out loud, three times each.

Success comes…when the mantras occur to you automatically during the day.

(Note, we have broken the 'Be Positive' mantras down into very small parts. It is important that we do not rush into seeking to acquire these. We want them to become a part of our psyche, and that cannot be rushed. Spend at least a week getting to the final stage of 'Be Positive' mantras.) You can write down the mantras on a table similar to the one below.

MANTRA (SAMPLE): I AM STRONG
MANTRA 1: _____
MANTRA 2: _____
MANTRA 3: _____
MANTRA 4: _____
MANTRA 5: _____

Drill 7: Mantra – Be Positive (2)

The Drill: Increase the mantras to ten, changing any that, on reflection, do not feel quite right. Learn them off by heart.

Success comes…when you have learned the mantras, and your mind is not thinking of new ones. In other words, you are happy that you have caught the self-motivation important for yourself. Try a table similar to the one below.

MANTRA (SAMPLE): I AM STRONG
MANTRA 1: _____
MANTRA 2: _____
MANTRA 3: _____
MANTRA 4: _____
MANTRA 5: _____
MANTRA 6: _____
MANTRA 7: _____
MANTRA 8: _____
MANTRA 9: _____
MANTRA 10: _____

Drill 8: Mantra – Be Positive (3)

The Drill: Begin each training or competition/match session by repeating the mantras to yourself three times.

Success comes…when we remember to carry out the task automatically, without having to remind ourselves.

Drill 9: Mantra – Be Positive (4)

The Drill: train ourselves, through repetition, to say the most relevant mantra three to five times at any pressure point during our sporting activities.

Success comes when we are able to do this in training so that we do it, without thinking, in the match or competition scenario. We can then reassess our mantra and adapt it as and when this is needed.

Laser Lock: Lou Gehrig's Trick to Ignoring the Noise and Nailing the Play

Avoiding Distraction And Focus on the task

We head further back in time for this chapter in order to encounter a baseball player whom many still consider to be the greatest of all time. Lou Gehrig. Simply consider some of the stats garnered during his career.

He is a member of the incredible Yankees' vintage of 1927, widely considered the greatest team of all time. Gehrig became the first player in the last century to hit four home runs in a game; a feat still so incredibly rare at professional level it has been achieved by only a handful of exponents. Still in his early twenties he breaks the longest consecutive games-played run, his 1308th match on the trot surpassing that of Everett Scott. And remember, this while being a part of a phenomenal Yankees team, almost any player of which would walk into an opponents' set up. He becomes the second player to reach 300 home runs – the first? The legendary Babe Ruth. He wins the triple crown, is pronounced by Time Magazine as the 'the game's No 1 batsman', a position, as we say, many believes he retains to this day,

So, a remarkable record – just a fraction of which we have touched upon above. But what does this have to do with focus, the subject of this chapter?

The answer, of course, is very much. Although we must reiterate that, as with every other elite athlete briefly biographized here, he holds every one of the mental strengths illustrated in this book, as well as remarkable physical attributes and skill. Mind you, that physique was not enough to win him the role of Tarzan, for which remarkably he auditioned as his baseball career was entering its twilight. The producer of the Edgar Rice Burrough's 'ape-man' classic describing Gehrig's legs as 'more functional than decorative'!

Firstly, there is the match day focus which every elite player of baseball requires, both in the field and when batting. The ball really does travel fast. That focus also had a safety element, to which we will return later. It is something that, certainly for non-players, does not really register in our thinking. We are used to seeing helmeted players enter the ballpark, well protected against the ball. This was not the case in Gehrig's day. Players rarely, if ever, wore helmets until the 1940s.

Inevitably, a player with such a reputation, and one who played so many consecutive games, was sometimes hit in the head. On one occasion at least, he was knocked unconscious for several minutes, although despite this turned out in the next day's game. Imagine the focus required for that! To know that you could be struck at any moment by a pitch you fractionally misread. To know that you could be rendered unconscious, or worse. Surely, for most of us, we would flinch – just a little. A fraction of our subconscious preparing to dodge. Our body position slightly altered; our mind slightly distracted. Not Gehrig. How do we know? Because of his continued incredible record.

We know much more about the importance of mental strength for athletes, as well as in every walk of life, these days. Back then, it rarely ever formed a part of a player's preparation. Basically, if you didn't have it, then you did not make it in elite sport, or if you broke through, you did not last long. So, from where might we trace Gehrig's focus? Possibly from his childhood. Henry Louis Gehrig (the 'Lou' came about as he shared his father's first name) was born into a tough childhood. Brought up in the rough district of East Harlem, money was tight. His parents are German immigrants – not easy in the New York of these days, so close to the end of the first world war – and his father is an alcoholic who is frequently out of work. His mother's work as a maid frequently provides the only income for the family. Gehrig is one of four siblings, but the only one to survive childhood. He is often found helping his mother out with her work.

Speaking only German at home, and for the first five years of his life, schoolwork becomes hard for the bilingual child. It often is for children who speak more than one language. Nevertheless, there is an indication of the focus he develops on achieving his goals in that he makes college. Although his studies there prove too much, and once more he commits totally to his athletic goals, this time seeking, and achieving, a career in sport.

There is, of course, famously, one last, tragic, element to Gehrig's story. One which further illustrates the strength of his focus to get him through adversity, as well as holding a particular relevance for today.

That is, tragically, the amyotrophic lateral sclerosis which ended his career early, and killed him two years later. It gained the pseudonym 'Gehrig's Disease', such was the name Lou Gehrig so worthy of high profile in the pre-war United States.

Gehrig had enjoyed a phenomenal season in 1937, despite inevitably suffering from the early stages of whatever was about to curtail both his career and his life. Again, demonstrating his remarkable ability to focus on the task at hand, to the exclusion of all else. The following season he noticed that he was exhausted by mid-season, and beginning to struggle with his power hitting and his famed speed between bases. Yet once more he pulls through, in the end achieving an above average season. By 1939, though, his physical decline has gained the upper hand. The focus remains, a journalist of the time notes that his technique is as perfect as ever, just his power has left him. He is due to play in a match against the Detroit Tigers when he tells his coach he is benching himself for the good of his team. He will never play a professional game again.

It is only many years after his death that the probability of Gehrig suffering from CTE, or chronic traumatic encephalopathy emerges. The disease is becoming a talking point in many contact sports around the world – football, rugby, even soccer with the concussive impact of heading soccer balls. There is nothing conclusive as to whether Gehrig did contract this disease, although his medical records show many old fractures to the skull. However, Gehrig had been cremated, and a diagnosis on records alone proved impossible.

None of this, of course, takes away from the fact that Gehrig is a sporting great, and one whose mental strength and focus contributed significantly to all he achieved.

We can all learn from Gehrig's focus. Focusing on a single task is one of those things that most people don't learn at school. As a result, we see that most people not only struggle to complete tasks, they also have a tendency to multi-task instead of staying in the moment. Focus is however a skill that one can build on over time. Here's a few drills you can work on to improve your mental focus.

Drill 10: In the Now

Dwelling on the past or overthinking the future takes attention away from the task at hand. Watch a soccer player take a penalty. See the focusing, the deep breath before striding forward to score. This is a form of **mindfulness.** The players are centering themselves in the now.

The Drill: Take yourself to a quiet location. Close your eyes and focus on your breathing. Count your breath in, and breathe out, and label them 1-10. Repeat.

When your mind begins to wander bring yourself back to your breathing.

Success comes...when you can center yourself through your breathing in any stressful situation.

Drill 11: Walking for Strength

Another **mindfulness** exercise. This drill offers the added bonus of physical exercise of walking.

The Drill: As before, concentrate on your breathing but this time as you walk. You will notice your senses become more alert. At the end of the walk tell yourself or write down twenty things you have observed. Time yourself doing this, to give a measure with which you compare your attentiveness.

Success comes…when you can remember the twenty items quickly and without difficulty. The ability to use all senses to absorb the multiple actions and interactions of any sport makes an athlete better.

You can write down the items in the space in the Figure below.

THINGS I NOTICED ON MY WALK

Item 1:   Item 2:

Item 3:   Item 4:

Item 5:   Item 6:

Item 7:   Item 8:

Item 9:   Item 10:

Item 11:   Item 12:

Item 13:   Item 14:

Item 15:   Item 16:

Item 17:   Item 18:

Item 19:   Item 20:

Drill 12: The Dress Rehearsal

It is the unexpected that catches us out. Admittedly, in sport we cannot prepare for every eventuality. But we can prepare for most. We do so with **visualization**. When Serena Williams goes through her serve routine, she is picturing exactly where her serve will land. She has done so tens of thousands of times. More often than not, she gets it right.

The Drill: We love our sport, or we wouldn't play it. So, it is no chore to picture scenarios in our head. Where will our pass go? How will we intercept? What force do we put on the ball to make that pass or score that goal?

Success comes…when our actions become automatic under the pressure of a game.

Drill 13: Focus on Coach

Allow our attention to drift no more than three times when the coach is speaking to the group.

Drill 14: 'A' for Achievable

Just as we wouldn't expect a fourteen-year-old sprinter to break the world 100m record, our mental goals also need to be realistic. Not stupidly easy, just something we can do.

The Drill: Focus on our breathing before beginning whatever action we are about to undertake.

Success comes...when we do this automatically, and do not have to think about it.

Success comes...well, that's pretty obvious.

Drill 15: The Mental MRI – 'M' for Meditate

The next three drills link to **meditation**. It will take a bit of practice to acquire the focus and skills to gain success with this activity but once achieved it will help your body to relax, and a relaxed athlete is a better athlete.

The Drill: Firstly, learn to meditate on your body. Start with the toes on your left foot (right foot, if you are left footed – we are beginning with the point of your body furthest from your brain.) Slowly focus on this point of your body until all other thoughts are gone. Work up your foot then your leg. Repeat for the other foot. Then move up your waist, stomach and chest. Same with your back. Work down each arm, then into your neck and then into your head.

Success comes…when you can meditate on all of your body without losing focus.

Drill 16: Mental MRI – 'R' for Reflect:

Once you have mastered the meditation element train your mind to reflect on each part of your body.

The Drill: Reflect on each part of your body, noting tension or discomfort. Note, it is important NOT to try to explain the discomfort. Just accept it.

Success comes…when you have trained your mind to accept any discomfort without judgement or assessment of the cause.

Drill 17: Mental MRI – 'I' for Initiate:

Initiate relaxation, that is.

The Drill: As you reach a part of your body with tension or discomfort, breathe out slowly, concentrating on relaxing that specific part of your body. Repeat twice more.

Success comes…when you can complete the body scan and feel more relaxed.

Drill 18: Breathe for Brilliance

We talk about the importance of breathing in many places during this chapter. Here, we aim to make breathing our dominant thought, which will help both relaxation and focus.

The Drill: Simply stand, lie or sit. Close your eyes. Breathe long and slowly in and out. Think only of your breathing. If your mind drifts onto something else, take a longer breath and bring it back.

Success comes…when you can focus for five minutes solely on breathing without your mind wandering.

Drill 19: Physical Locks

Ever seen a soccer player pull their socks up? A basketball player clap their hands? Chances are they are enacting a physical lock. An action to get their focus back on track.

The Drill: Decide on a short but simple action which works for you. Ensure it might not be interpreted negatively by a teammate, but otherwise it can be anything from scratching your head to one of the above. Practice in various situations, not just sporting ones, doing the action, and refocusing (perhaps using one of the breathing drills to help gain this.) Then, employ it in your athletic situations.

Success comes…when you can do the action and find your focus has returned.

Drill 20: Verbal Locks

Just like the physical lock, but this time develop a phrase, word or sound which triggers your focus. There is no need to have both, but you might want to experiment with physical and verbal locks to see which works best.

The Drill: As above using verbal cue.

Success comes… as above.

Drill 21: Maximizing the Warm-Up

It is easy to think of the warmup as purely physical training, getting our muscles ready and easing tensions from our bodies. This is partly true, but it is a good opportunity to develop focus as well.

The Drill: Consciously concentrate on every warm-up activity, considering why you are doing it, and how best to do it. This will help develop your mental focus.

Success comes…when you are so prepared for the warm-up that you do not need the drill.

Eyes on the Prize: Niki Lauda's Masterclass in Ditching Instant Wins for Epic Long-Term Goals

Self-Discipline – Long-term Goals Over Short-Term Gains

There's no sport, certainly not mainstream sport, which carries more danger for the world's leading participants than motor racing. Formula One sits at the top of the list of sports requiring extreme bravery as well as extreme skill, technique, physical fitness and mental strength.

It is August 1st, 1976, and the West German Grand Prix is running on the famous Nurburgring track. Niki Lauda is probably the greatest driver of that era, although there is plenty of competition. Safety levels, both for the tracks and the cars which hare around them, are certainly better than they were twenty years before (fifteen drivers lost their lives in the 1950s compared to a still appalling twelve in the 1970s), but nothing like the levels of safety present today, where the cockpit is a rigid cocoon of protection. Indeed, it has been more than a decade since Jules Bianchi lost his life at the Japanese Grand Prix. That was back in 2014.

Lauda is leading the world championship table but starts second on the grid behind his closest challenger, the British driver James Hunt. Lauda, driving a Ferrari, is hurling his car around the track when it loses traction, swerves off the tarmac and hits a wall, bouncing back onto the track just as the chasing cars reach the spot.

The car bursts immediately into flames, and to make matters worse two fellow drivers – Harald Ertl and Brett Lunger – crash into it. Both the horror of the occasion, and the camaraderie of the league of ultra-competitive drivers shows itself. Remember, one of the vital mental strengths of top athletes is perspective. Ertl and Brett leap from their cars, and two other drivers scream to a halt. The British driver Guy Edwards and the Italian Arturo Merzario pull themselves out of their vehicles and all four rush to their colleague's rescue. Guy Edwards related later the problems they encountered in freeing Lauda. Reported on the BBC's 'On the Day' webpage, he says 'Lauda was basically sitting in the middle of a fire, and I would guess it would be about a minute before we managed to get the belts undone.'

Lauda is still conscious, shouting for the drivers to get him out. Ertl manages to locate an extinguisher, and after around a minute of struggling, the drivers release him from the burning wreck, where he is cradled, dying, by another driver, John Watson, until medical assistance arrives.

He is taken to the nearest hospital, but his injuries are beyond what the Adenau hospital can treat, his burns so serious that, despite being flown to the major University Hospital in Mannheim, it seems certain that Lauda will not survive his injuries. He is given the last rites at the hospital.

Six weeks later Niki Lauda is once more behind the wheel of his Formula One racing car. Something Watson describes as the bravest thing he has ever seen. It is hard to conceive of the self-discipline required for such action. Fortunately, most of us will not face life or death situations; even fewer will, like Lauda, find themselves close to death because of your own sport. Yet Lauda puts it all behind him, gets back behind the wheel, overcomes whatever inevitable doubts must have entered his head. Eschews the benefits and pleasures of an instant and understandable retirement. For mortals like us, it might be hard to understand why. Even tougher to conceive of how. But Niki Lauda has that mental strength to return to his car.

Lauda's motivation, he says, was to get back to winning the world championship from his great rival and even greater friend, James Hunt. He doesn't succeed in 1976 but lifts the title in 1977.

He bears the physical scars of his crash for the rest of his life, most notably the scar tissue on his face and forehead.

Who knows what physical and, perhaps even more significant, psychological pain Lauda endured in getting back into his car. He already had a world title, won in 1975, (He gains his third in 1984). Every fellow driver, Formula One fan, commentator and decent human being would hold the utmost respect for Lauda had he decided to call it a day following the crash, perhaps moving more quickly into other aspects of the sport, as he did after his eventual retirement. He would be a legend whatever his decision back in the summer of '76. Yet he foregoes the totally understandable and still extremely brave decision to retire from his sport, at least at the level of a driver, in order to pursue his longer-term goals of lifting another world championship. Perhaps continuing for many more seasons after he ultimately fails to lift the Drivers' Championship in 1976 is just as brave, just as much evidence of his determination to follow his long-term goals, as is getting back into his car in the first place.

Lauda's is an extreme example of pursuing one's long-term ambitions whilst eschewing short term wins. Nevertheless, it provides powerful evidence of the ability the very best athletes in their sport hold to achieve this challenging goal.

While we hopefully will never have to deal with the kind of pain and turmoil Niki Lauda had to, we can still work on our Self-Discipline daily to ensure that we work towards our long-term goals. Now, let's have a look at some drills that will improve our Self-Discipline.

Drill 22: The Cold Start Drill

Goal: Train yourself to take action without needing motivation.

Drill: Pick a physically demanding activity (e.g., sprints, burpees, or pushups).

Do it first thing in the morning, without warm-up, hype, or music.

The rule:

Start within 2 minutes of waking up — no excuses.

Why it works:

Builds the habit of acting without negotiating with your feelings.

Drill 23: Distraction Kill Drill

Goal: Strengthen focus and impulse control.

How it works:

Choose a focused task (film study, meditation, journaling, etc.).

Put your phone in another room — or use app blockers.

Set a timer for **30–45 minutes** of deep focus, no breaks.

Gradually increase to 90+ minutes.

Why it works: Trains your brain to resist dopamine distractions.

Drill 24: In-competition sensory support

We can, though, use our senses to help instill calmness during in-competition action. A calm and relaxed mind is more likely to be disciplined during a match.

The Drill: Use the most appropriate sense for the environment. These will mostly be sight or hearing but can be any. Focus solely on that sense during play. For example, the sound of fellow runners' feet hitting the track.

Success comes…when the drill quickly helps us feel more relaxed and focused.

Drill 25: Mindfulness with Nutrition

Perhaps the single biggest change in the way elite athletes perform nowadays is connected to their diet. The one part of our life where discipline is most needed, where there is no coach to supervise us, is our diet.

The Drill: As we eat, focus on the taste of each chew, the texture in our mouths and the sensation as we swallow. This slows down our eating and helps us focus. Nutritionally, eating slowly and chewing also helps us with better digestion.

Success comes…when we note we are eating more slowly.

Swagger Central: Tiger Woods' Blueprint for Believing You're the Boss

Confidence – Belief in One's Ability to Succeed

True, Tiger Woods is one of those athletes who split opinion. There are those that love his confidence, his self-belief. There are those who feel he has gone too far, particularly in his life outside of golf. Others again who sense that bad luck has befallen him.

But what few will disagree with is that his is a phenomenal talent. Probably, he is the greatest golfer the planet has ever seen. And, really, are there any but the toughest hearts who don't secretly (or openly) hope he will secure one more major before age and his failing frame force his final, permanent retirement?

'Tiger's vision has always been focused beyond – beyond expectations, beyond comparisons, and beyond limits.' These are the opening words of the 'Founder's Story' element of his website. True, very probably. Needing to be said, in writing…part of a website? Well, that will depend on your own view of the man.

We've focused perhaps more than we should on Woods' personality and character. Indeed, far more than with other legendary sports players in this book to date. But this is for a reason. When it comes to self-confidence, it is something that exists within us, or does not.

So, when Woods tells his father that he will become someone 'professionally excellent' – and the numerous showings of a very young Tiger striking a golf ball using a club so long that he can only hold it at an angle of forty-five degrees - tells us that he is referring to only one thing with those words. His future golfing career. (Note: for clarification, this section of the website is headed 'off the course'.)

Woods, by the way, is nine years old when he makes that prediction to his father.

A prediction that turns out to be true. Woods secures, to date, eighty-two victories in PGA Tour events. With 18 World Golf championships, he is the only modern times player to be victorious in four consecutive major titles. He has won two players championships, and perhaps most notably, fifteen major championships.

Such success undoubtedly requires every mental strength identified in this book. But perhaps self-belief is the most important, especially in a sport such as golf. It is hard to think of any comparable sport which provides such an opportunity for the mind to get in the way of the body. Most sport contains a large element of instinct, of thinking too fast to rationalize. Maybe the cue sports – snooker, pool and billiards – provide similar challenges, although golf adds a physical requirement to the repertoire.

Uncontrolled nerves lead to tension and faults with grip or swing. Distractions might lead to the miniscule error in striking point that dispatches the ball tens of meters off course, perhaps landing in the rough. A strategically and skillfully situated bunker or the water feature adds to the beauty of the course but spoils the round of the unwary. Thinking of your opponents is inevitable – in some sports it is important – but in golf it can only serve to distract from your own game. Because again golf is one of the very few sports where the play of your opponent rarely, if ever, directly influences your own game.

All of this leads to the firm requirement for phenomenal self-belief. A player must have complete confidence that they are, on the day, the best player there. The one capable of meeting any challenges. The one with the best plan for tackling the course and the conditions. The one who, when the pressure putt is faced, will keep calm and bury the ball.

Woods, along with all super-elite athletes, has this. It is one of those characteristics that sets him apart.

It is important, though, to separate self-belief from over confidence. Indeed, on the website mentioned earlier, another of Woods' maxims is highlighted. This maxim states that one of the joys of his life is the knowledge that in everything you do, you can always be better. Constructive self-criticism – recognizing your strengths and achievements whilst at the same time understanding what you can do to be better still – is an essential part of being the best athlete that you can be. It is a trait that fits perfectly with self-confidence. The point at which you feel you are simply as good as anybody can be is the point at which you begin to stand still, that others catch you up and surpass you.

It is stated earlier in the chapter that self-belief is something that comes from within. This is true. There is undoubtedly a touch of (necessary) arrogance about the very best athletes. But, hey, don't such people have plenty to be a little arrogant about? Yet, these athletes –

such as Tiger Woods – also hold some humility. They recognize that they are just a part of their sports history, not the whole of it. They understand that in the future there will be players with new skills, new strengths, better training, even ones who achieve more success. But, that is fine, because like all the best athletes, they also live in the now. Not the time to come, or the time that has passed. Their confidence comes in part from the knowledge that they have worked as hard as they currently can, have prepared as well as they currently can and are as ready as they currently can be.

Tiger Woods has the confidence… the self-belief not just to think he is the best but to know that he is the best, and so he becomes the best. Of course, this confidence is matched by astonishing ability – sadly simply believing we are better than everybody else will not make us so, although doubting we can win will frequently lead to defeat.

So, here is a tip. If you have self-belief as a part of your psychological make up, that is wonderful and as long as it is tempered by its partners of humility and a knowledge that you can become even better still, it is a great trait to possess. If self-confidence is not a natural part of your make-up, then do the following things:

Firstly, ask yourself why, and when you reach the answer, address it if it needs to be addressed, and if it is something that you cannot change, dismiss it. Otherwise, it will only hold you back.

Secondly, work, train, study as hard as you can. Then, over time, that self-belief will begin to emerge. Nothing promotes it more than success, and hard work is the key to such success.

Now, let's try and improve our confidence in the real world.

Drill 26: Know Yourself

It should be clear now that the major barriers to having mental strength in sporting situations are the things that distract us from it. In other words, the elements within ourselves make it difficult for us to use the mental strength characteristics we describe in detail in this book. The first step to achieving confidence is to understand ourselves completely. If need be, you can revisit this drill after you complete the entire book.

The Drill: A useful exercise, to complete over eight to ten short sessions, is to take each of the mental toughness elements one at a time and write down what stops us from being as good as we can be in that particular area. For example, we might write: 'Resilience – I feel it is my fault when the team loses,' or 'Self-Discipline – when the race gets close at the end, I feel my muscles getting tight, and I focus on this rather than my strategy.' We then revisit these concerns, adapting them as needed. You can start off in the space below or in your own notebook/journal if you need more space. It can be useful, for ease of finding them, to either have a couple of pages in your journal dedicated to this topic, or to color code them. Use pictures or symbols if you prefer to work that way. It is YOUR notebook. Success comes…when we are self-aware of what might cause us to have a barrier to mental strength. Knowing the problem makes it easier to overcome.

Area 1: Resilience

What Prevents Me from Having Resilience:

Area 2: Focus

What Prevents Me from having Focus

Area 3: Self Discipline

What Prevents Me from Having Self-Discipline

Area 4: Confidence

What Prevents Me from Having Confidence

Area 5: Mental Flexibility

What Prevents Me from Having Mental Flexibility:

Area 6: Intrinsic Motivation

What Makes Me Lose Motivation

Area 7: Optimism

What Makes Me Pessimistic

Area 8: Emotional Regulation

What Prevents Me from Regulating My Emotions

Drill 27: Be Your Favorite Mentor

Think about the best teacher you have ever had. Or, if that is tough, perhaps the best sports coach (although there is likely to be a smaller pool here.)

The Drill: Write down the traits of this person which made you like them. Probably, on the list, there will be words and phrases like: 'respects me', 'likes me', 'fun', 'calm but with authority'…those sorts of words. Phrases unlikely to appear are 'shouts a lot', 'unfair', 'harsh', 'never praises'. These are likely qualities that you admire and also help you improve your confidence. The person we talk to most is ourselves. So we can start talking to ourselves in the way that our favorite coach talks to us.

Success comes…when you learn to respect yourself. High standards and positive criticism are fine, but within the context of the positivity your best ever teacher generates. Write down the 5 qualities you like best about the person below.

Name of Favorite Mentor:

Role of Favorite Mentor:

Quality 1:

Quality 2:

Quality 3:

Quality 4:

Quality 5:

Drill 28: Win the First Hour Drill

Goal: Create momentum and belief in your ability to follow through.

Drill: Start each day with a structured routine that includes:

Movement (e.g., light cardio or stretching)

Mental focus (e.g., journaling or breathwork)

One small task that contributes to your goals

Track your streak. Aim for consistency, not perfection.

Why it works: Builds identity — *"I'm someone who gets things done."* That fuels confidence.

Drill 29: Pressure Simulation Drill

Goal: Build confidence under stress by replicating real performance conditions.

Drill: Recreate high-stakes scenarios in training (e.g., last-minute free kick, match point, final lap).

Add pressure: Countdowns, peer eyes on you, or consequences for mistakes.

Practice performing while feeling nerves.

Why it works: Confidence grows when you repeatedly prove to yourself you can handle pressure.

Drill 30: Daily Micro-Wins Log

Goal: Focus the mind on progress and success, not flaws.

Drill: Every day, write down 3 small wins — no matter how minor.

Examples: Nailed your nutrition, hit your sprint target, kept calm after a mistake. Review weekly to track growth.

Why it works: Shifts your focus from what's missing to what's improving — builds self-trust. Get started in the space below and eventually switch to your notebook.

Day 1 Date:

Win 1:

Win 2:

Win 3:

Day 2 Date:

Win 1:

Win 2:

Win 3:

Drill 31: Self Evaluate Our Strategy

We won't get it right straight away. Use our journal to note down the pluses and minuses of our strategy in a competitive situation. We will then be able to retain the elements which work, whilst adapting those which do not.

The Drill and success criteria…as above.

This Drill helps you build confidence in your strategy as you refine it with your analysis.

Describe Strategy:

Benefits of Strategy 1:

Benefits of Strategy 2:

Benefits of Strategy 3:

Drawbacks of Strategy 1:

Drawbacks of Strategy 2:

Modified Strategy considering Benefits/Drawbacks:

Reward 2:

As a reward for reading this chapter on confidence, we wanted to give you a bonus that you will enjoy. It's a list of mental affirmations that you can recite daily to improve your confidence.

A Short message from the Author:

Hey, are you enjoying the book? I'd love to hear your thoughts!

Many readers do not know how hard reviews are to come by, and how much they help an author.

I would be incredibly thankful if you could take just 60 seconds to write a brief review on Amazon, even if it's just a few sentences!

Your review will genuinely make a difference for me and help gain exposure for my work.

Curveball King: John McEnroe's Art of Thinking Fast and Flipping the Script

Mental Flexibility – The Ability to be Creative and Adapt when Circumstances Dictate

Men's professional tennis is seeing one of the golden periods of the game come to pass. From the point that Mark Philippoussis saw his dreams of Wimbledon glory dissipate beneath the gilded onslaught of the new kid on the block, Roger Federer, in 2003 until Novak Djokovic once more lifted the US Open in 2023, five men, with three in particular, dominated the game. Who is to say that Djokovic doesn't have another grand slam in him?

In fact, incredibly, of the sixty-four grand slams played between 2005 and 2019 only three were won by a player outside of the top five in the world. Marat Safin (Australian) in 2005, Juan Martin Del Potro (US) in 2009 and Marin Cilic (US) in 2014. Stan Wawrinka and Andy

Murray lifted three titles each during that period…and you have to feel a little sorry for these great players. In any other era, they would dominate the game (in fact Murray spent nearly a year as world number one). The other grand slams in this period were shared between Novak Djokovic (career total 24), Rafael Nadal (22) and Roger Federer (20). In fact, these three – all in their thirties by now, lifted eleven of the fifteen grand slams (one being cancelled due to Covid 19) played between 2020 and 2023.

It was not always so. Before a mixture of racket technology, nutrition and training turned the game into such a power-dominated sport, players tended to gain particular success in one or two of the grand slam surfaces. In fact, only four players prior to Andre Agassi in the nineties won all four titles during their career, although in those days three of the tournaments took place on grass.

Then, in 1974 Bjorn Borg, the mighty and metronomic Swede, won the French Open. Two years later he was victorious on the grass of

Wimbledon. He would go on to win in the southwest of London for five consecutive years. Including defeating John McEnroe in five grueling, almighty sets in 1980. The following year, McEnroe recovers to beat Borg on Centre court at Wimbledon. When he defeats the same player at the US open later that year, Borg, just twenty-six, decides to call it a day and retires from the sport.

McEnroe's success is built on a mixture of physical prowess, astonishing technique, and great mental resilience. But there is more. There is an intellect about McEnroe, a study and knowledge of the game, a willingness to improvise, to play the drop shot when others would not, to volley when others would stay back, to outthink his opponents through a detailed, studious analysis of their game. It is an approach which marks him out. It is no wonder that he has gone on to become an outstanding analyst and pundit on the game.

McEnroe's unorthodox game, with precision volleys, touch and serve and volley tactics, required mental flexibility to adapt to opponents and match conditions. The baseline heavy power game of his rivals Bjorn Borg and Jimmy Connors were in contrast to the finesse of McEnroe. McEnroe constantly adjusted to his opponent's strategies, surfaces, and match situation.

In the 1980 Wimbledon final against Borg, which he lost, McEnroe showcased a lot of mental flexibility in staying mentally engaged against Borg. He adapted an aggressive net play against Borg's powerful and consistent baseline game. McEnroe changed his tactics mid-match, implementing variations in his service placement and precise passing shots. These strategies allowed him to outclass players like Connors and Borg over the next few years. This resulted in his 1984 being an Open era record, with an 82-3 win record.

John McEnroe is a fine example of the power of adaptability, creativity and dictating circumstance, rather than allowing it to dominate him, that marks out the greatest sports players. Would John McEnroe have still been a great tennis player without the mental flexibility he possessed? Very probably. Would he have become the best in the world, have won numerous grand slams? Probably not.

We can use John McEnroe as an example in our daily lives and think of ways to improve our performance by changing strategies. There are some drills that can help with this.

Drill 32: Scenario Switch Up

Objective: Enhance adaptability to unexpected changes.

Drill: This can be adapted to any drill that you are doing for your sport of choice. In the middle of the drill, change the rules or conditions of the drill. For example, in a baseball scrimmage, switch from a full game to a "one-pitch" format where each batter gets only one pitch to hit. Encourage kids to adjust strategies on the fly without complaining.

Why it works: Simulates unpredictable game situations, fostering flexibility.

Duration: 10-15 minutes, 1-2 times per practice.

Also note that this drill works best if the kids are in a comfort zone, and their skills have got to a flat line, where they are decently good at the techniques of the sports they are performing.

Drill 33: Rule Switch Scrimmage

Objective: Train athletes to adapt to sudden rule changes.

Drill: During a scrimmage (e.g., soccer), pause every 10-15 minutes to change a rule (e.g., no passing with dominant foot, score only with headers). Athletes must adjust their playstyle immediately. Encourage quick huddles to discuss new strategies.

Why it works: Forces rapid cognitive shifts, mimicking unpredictable game moments.

Duration: 15-20 minutes per scrimmage.

This again works when the kids are in a comfort zone and need to expand on their skills.

Drill 34: The Eton Fives Conundrum

Ever seen Eton Fives played? Even heard of it? Probably not. Well, fives (there are three varieties which originated in the public schools of the United Kingdom) is an incredibly fast, skillful and entertaining sport. In simple terms it is squash played with a hard ball on an unusual court using gloved hands. Power, finesse, spin, two hands and bizarre rules. (Where else might a poor server be called a 'blackguard'?) At the highest level – say the Kinnaird Cup, the world championship, play is so fast it is hard to see the ball. So, the best practitioners are really very, very good. True elite sportsman. Are they professionals though? Not a chance. There is no money at all in this sport. And that is true of most of the sports ever created, Even in those in which it is possible to make a very, very good living – American Football, basketball, soccer, athletics, golf, tennis and so forth, only a tiny percentage of the best players go on to be professional, and even for those, bar the very, very best of the best, their living is a struggle.

Everything about this book is about positivity and success, and we never wish to crush a dream. If nobody tried to be an elite athlete, there would be none. But few succeed. So, for our general mental health, we say try, dream, aim high…but counter this by saying make sure that you never stop enjoying your sport, and always ensure there are other parts to your life.

The Drill: Research a lesser known sport, think about how much the players participate for the thrill of playing rather than the financial rewards of winning.

Success comes…when you find yourself playing solely because you enjoy it. For most readers, that will be their motivation in any case. Also, enjoying another sport will open your mind to new possibilities in your sport of choice. Athletes who play multiple sports are more likely to be mentally flexible as well and adapt better to different situations as well.

Drill 35: Beware the Coach who Lives through You

Another slight warning here, and we promise it is the last. After this drill it is back to the positive. Although, really, the warning which follows is also positive. Bear it in mind and happiness will almost certainly follow.

The Drill: Not really a drill, more a touch of advice. If you are struggling with your coach, speak to them, or if this is difficult, speak to a trusted friend or family member.

Success comes…whenever your relationship with your coach is one with which you feel completely comfortable.

Drill 36: Get Advice on the Strategy

We are building a position where we trust our strategies. Therefore, they must work for us. If our strategies consistently fail, we will not trust them.

The Drill: The best way to get a successful strategy is to take advice from your coach, or others in whom you have faith.

Success comes…when we have a good, two-way relationship with our advisor or coach regarding strategy.

Drill 37: **Honesty is the Only Policy** When it comes to Evaluating Our Strategy.

It is a natural human trait to blame. So, we might blame our strategy for running out of steam on the final length of our breaststroke race. But, of course, strategy is only one aspect of performance.

The Drill: The strategy you have developed could be very good, even if your match or event did not go as you hoped. So before blaming it (or indeed, any other factor) rationalize all elements of performance, including preparation. Did I train hard enough? Did I eat properly in the lead up to the event? Did I get enough sleep? Were my competitors simply better than me? It can help to write down our analysis of our performance.

Success comes…when we feel we are objectively analyzing our performance.

Fire in the Gut: Simone Biles' Deep-Down Drive to Crush It

Intrinsic Motivation – The Internal drive to achieve your Goals

According to many who know about these things, Simone Biles is the greatest gymnast of all time. Certainly, over three Olympic Games, from Rio in 2016 through to Paris in 2024, she won a remarkable eleven medals, and what is even more special about these is that no less than seven of these are gold. If that were not enough to mark her out as the greatest gymnast of her generation, and probably throughout the history of the sport, then she can add to that total:

- Twenty-three gold medals from the World Championships.
- Six World all-round titles.
- Twenty-seven US Championship golds over an incredible eleven years of competition.
- Twenty US Classic gold medals.

- Numerous golds at other international events.
- Silver and bronze medals at the highest level. (Less than her total of gold medals, largely because when she competes, she tends to take the top spot on the podium.)

In what is a young woman's sport, Simone Biles enjoyed a long career, competing until the age of twenty-seven and retiring at the peak of her powers, immediately after her 'come back' Olympics in Paris 2024. She took up the sport aged just six. To meet the training challenges alone of a twenty-one-year career requires immense intrinsic motivation just on its own. Yet perhaps one of her greatest strengths is her all-round mental prowess. Her honesty, ability to self-reflect, her sense of perspective, her inner strength, her inner strength, her inner strength, her inner strength, her focus are all of the highest level. But let us look at just one of these strengths. Her sense of perspective. Consider these words, which she said in 2023 on her return to the sport following a potentially career ending issue which came to the fore at the 2020 (held, due to Covid-19, in 2021) Olympic Games in Tokyo:

'Gymnastics is something that I do, and it's not who I am as a person, and I think it took years to realize that. It's kind of nice to break out of that shell.'

This chapter uses Simone Biles to illustrate the importance of deep, inner drive. Yet like so many of the athletes we use as examples in this book, Simone achieves that drive despite a series of deeply challenging circumstances in her life. There are three, perhaps four challenges, in particular which she overcomes, and to do so and become possibly the greatest gymnast of all time is a measure of the inner belief and motivation she must hold.

Firstly, Simone's early childhood is not easy. She is the third of four brothers and sisters, but as a baby her mother struggles to look after her young family. Like many in such difficult situations, Simone and her siblings find themselves in the uncertain world of foster care. Then, in 2000 when Simone is still a toddler, her maternal grandfather, Ron, and his wife begin to look after the children.

It is a more stable environment for the bubbly young child, and indeed Ron and his wife Nellie will go on to become significant figures in both Simone's personal life and her career. However, in 2003 the decision is taken that Ron and Nellie will adopt Simone and her younger sibling, whilst his sister, Harriet, will adopt the two older siblings. Whilst essential stability comes into Simone's life, her family is split up. A challenge she will overcome with her grandparents' and now adoptive parents' support.

The second major challenge to Simone Biles' personal life and career is also potentially not only career destroying, but life destroying. Sadly, in a very small percentage of cases, coaches and trainers do not enter their career with the right intentions, or if they do, they allow their own personal weaknesses to become dominant. We read frequently, too frequently, of stories of youth athletes being abused by, usually, men they should be able to trust.

This happens to Simone. The former doctor to USA gymnastics, Larry Nassar, would be convicted of sexually assaulting a number of female gymnasts. One of his victims is Simone Biles. To add salt to this painful wound, many of Nassar's victims testified that the abuse was known about within the USA gymnastics set up and covered up. A story heard about too often across sports. Another horrendous challenge that Simone Biles overcomes.

Finally, among these major challenges to her personal life and career, comes one which threatens to directly end that career. Having swept the board, just about, at Rio in the 2016 Olympics, Simone Biles lifts a couple of medals at the Tokyo Olympics in 2021. But she is nothing like at her best. She has to withdraw from a number of events. It turns out that she is suffering from a mental condition called 'The Twisties'; this fundamentally causes gymnasts to lose control of their position in the air during the complex routines. Put simply, in the middle of a mid-air twisting or tumbling combination, the gymnast does not know where she or he is.

Yet, such is the mental strength and self-belief of Simone Biles that she still achieves a bronze at this, the highest level of competition, on that most tricky of apparatus, the beam. Imagine that, with a sense of position and awareness lost through no fault of your own, such are your skills that you are still the third best in the world on an apparatus four inches wide. One from which a fall could easily break an ankle, or worse.

In fact, just two days before the final Simone's aunt dies, unexpectedly, and she feels she must perform. Despite the many golds, to Simone this is the most meaningful medal she ever wins.

And from this potentially career ending illness, Simone Biles's motivation and inner drive is such that, just three years later, at the Paris Olympics, she is once again undisputedly the world's greatest gymnast.

No doubt, some of that motivation came from external factors – coaches, colleagues, family and such like. But to overcome such challenges as she faced throughout her career, Simone must hold a further type of motivation, a very important one. Intrinsic motivation. That motivation within yourself to overcome whatever stands in your way and achieve all that you possibly can. Even in the face of extreme adversity. To overcome that adversity, as Simone Biles has done (certainly in the professional sense) requires incredible motivation, and such is the personal trauma she has suffered that this motivation can surely only come from within.

While a lot of intrinsic motivation comes from within, most athletes and people are not connected with their purpose. So they're not as motivated as they can be. This is a detriment to achieving their goals. However, we can work on a few drills to help you get better connected to your goals and achieve intrinsic motivation.

Drill 38: 'T' is for Timed Limit on Goals

There is no rush to achieve our goals, but we do need a deadline. Or, a goal will just drift along. Nobody likes moving goalposts! The first step to being motivated is to set a time limit for our goals

The Drill: I will improve my fitness at the beginning of pre-season training by increasing my bleep test (repeated timed running between markers) by 10% within one week. For example, in the first session I achieve ten short runs within the time, after a week I can do eleven.

Success comes…when we automatically set a limit in which we must achieve the goal.

Drill 39: Personal Goal

This one is prepared beforehand and used in a training session. Our coach will often set team or personal objectives for a session. To this we add one of our own. Something SMART. Just one. That's important, or we can become overwhelmed and achieve little.

The Drill: Set a personal objective. For example, a basketball player may seek to shoot 90% of his free throws within 3 months. Success comes…when we are able to focus on our personal goal, as well as those set by our coaches. Write down your personal goal below so you can reference it at a future date.

Describe Goal:

Now, let's adjust this goal to make it SMART:

S (Specific): Make the goal specific. What exactly do you want to achieve?

M (Measurable): Make sure it is quantifiable. E.g. Run 100 m in 12 seconds instead of "Run As fast As I can"

A (Achievable): Is it Achievable? Make sure it is achievable for you in the time frame you mention below.

R (Relevant): Make sure it is relevant to your sport. E.g. If you're a sprinter, don't make a swimming goal

T (Time Bound): Make sure you set a time to achieve your goal. E.g., Run 100 m in 12 seconds within 6 months.

SMART Goal: Describe your SMART Goal Now based on what you wrote before:

E.g. Run 100m in 12 seconds within 6 months. I currently run 100 m in 15 seconds.

Drill 40: The "Why 5x" Drill

Goal: Discover deeper internal reasons for training or competing.

Drill:

- Write down a goal (e.g., "I want to make varsity.")
- Ask: "Why do I want that?"
- Take your answer and ask "Why?" again — do this 5 times.
- By the 5th level, you'll usually hit a core value like pride, belonging, mastery, or passion.

Why it works: Clarifies personal purpose — the foundation of intrinsic motivation.

SMART Goal: _____

Why 1: Why are you pursuing this goal?

Why 2: Why?

Why 3? Why?

Why 4? Why?

Why 5? Why?

Sunshine Superpower: Jesse Owens' Positivity Hack to Leap Over Life's Hurdles

Optimism – A Positive Mindset to Help Surmount Obstacles, Overcome Adversity and Maintain Perspective

It was a different world in 1936. Certainly, current political unrest suggests it was not quite as different as we might want it to be, but nevertheless, the rise of an evil, right-wing dictator is threatening world peace. Within three more years, he will destroy that world peace and create a global conflict that will lead to the deaths of millions. In doing so, he will attempt to eradicate a people from the planet.

It is in the face of such tyranny, hatred and wickedness that a person may take on legendary proportions. Jesse Owens is one such man. Without doubt, Owens is one of the most famous sporting heroes in history. Perhaps second only to the great Muhammed Ali, it is sometimes inevitable that the symbolism of his success in 1936 clouds his prowess as an athlete. As Adolf Hitler sought to use the Berlin Olympics as a propaganda machine to promote his view of the superiority, the dominance, of the Aryan race; Owen demonstrated the might of the African American athlete on the world stage.

If this chapter is about the importance of optimism, self-belief, the power to overcome adversity and the importance of maintaining perspective as you seek to achieve your goals, then Jesse Owens had it tougher than most.

James Cleveland Owens (the 'Jesse' originated from a teacher mis-hearing his known name – JC – and calling him Jesse) was the youngest of ten children born to Henry and Emma. His grandfather was a former slave. Life was tough for young Jesse, and money tight. But the fire and belief lay in his family. A trust that they can overcome the challenge they face. We mustn't over romanticize here; this is not a family – or a people – born with a rose tinted, bosom swelling desire to overcome adversity and represent their people, leading them to a new horizon. This is not some second-rate B list straight-to-TV film. This is reality. So, yes, there is a desire to overcome adversity, but that is because, simply, the family have to do that to survive.

But although money is tight, love and support are not. And so, when it begins to become apparent that Jesse is a rare talent on the track, he is supported in every way possible. But he is black, not white. And he is an athlete, not a baseball player. There is no sponsorship, no salary to allow him to train while living a comfortable life. As he enters his teenage years and early adulthood, Owens works a number of jobs to support himself enough to allow him to train. Despite the support of many, there is also opposition from more than a few. Owens' place of birth is Alabama, hardly, in those days, a hotbed of racial equality or opportunity for black people. In fact, along with his young wife Ruth he heads north to the University of Ohio, but despite his incredible talent, there is no scholarship for athletes of Owens' ilk in those days, and again he takes on a number of jobs to keep the two of them afloat. He stacks books in the library, pumps gas, works as a page, a waiter, and a night elevator operator.

All the time, often with little or no sleep, he tackles his studies, practices his sport and wins competition after competition.

In 1935 Owens enters the Big Ten Championships. He is carrying an injury at the time, having hurt his back in a fall (not, typically, one gained during training, but he has fallen down a flight of stairs.) Unsure whether he can compete, he enters the 100-yard dash, runs a time of 9.4 seconds and equals the world record. With an injury. To his back. Over the next 45 minutes he breaks three more world records in various events.

And so, in 1936, a black man, an American at that, travels to Europe to compete in Adolf Hitler's games. The blue riband event, then as now, is the men's sprint, and Owens wins that, as well as three other gold medals.

There is a famous and hugely telling photo of Owen atop the victory rostrum. The stadium in Berlin is filled with Nazi salutes, arms outstretched and pointing slightly upwards. A salute of pure evil. The officials surrounding the rostrum too stand with their arm raised. The most powerful part of all, however, is the subject of the photo. Jesse Owens stands higher than all, proud and with his arms by his side. Refusing to participate in the gesture. The silver medal winning athlete, also black, reflects Owens' position. Behind, and of course lower, the third-place athlete, Aryan in looks, raises his arm in the Nazi salute. The symbolism is clear. Naziism will not dominate. It might be another nine years before it is finally vanquished, with the Allied victory in World War II, and still, it festers like unwanted mold in the basement of a decaying home, but the image shows, it will not prevail.

Hitler, of course, fails to acknowledge Owens' success.

After the Olympics Jesse Owens commits to a life of supporting the underprivileged children in particular. Doing good. Helping, supporting, giving opportunity.

Surmounting obstacles? Remaining positive? Overcoming adversity? Maintaining perspective. Jesse Owens exemplifies all of these traits.

We may not all become elite athletes in our sport, we probably won't become Olympic gold medalists. But if we wish to enjoy our sport to its maximum degree, and achieve all that we can, then there is no better role model to inspire us than Jesse Owens. Perhaps we can take from the great man one aspect of mental strength more than any other. That being his optimism. His belief that he will get through the impossible challenges of working full time jobs while undertaking full time training. That he can still win when he is subject, like Muhammed Ali as we saw earlier, to intense personal prejudice. That of his love of running and jumping. His commitment to them. These can, for a while at least, even overcome the power of the most evil dictator the world has ever seen.

That, my friends, is optimism. And when, like Jesse Owens, you possess such optimism then anything is possible.

While nobody is born with a sense of optimism, it can be built over time by working on our mindset. Let's look at a few drills to fuel our optimism:

Drill 41: Retaking the Picture

Negative thoughts can get us down. They ruin our confidence, challenge our self-belief, make us lose motivation. We miss two consecutive back hands on the court, our backhand is a liability. We drop the ball in the field. We can't catch.

But we can retake that picture, make it a positive rather than a negative. 'If I get into position more quickly, my backhand will improve.' 'I did really well to get into position where I could at least get my hand on that chance, next time I will catch it.'

Retaking the picture is something we see widely among elite athletes. Errors do not get them down. They recognize them and determine how to improve next time.

The Drill: Each day write down two things that have happened, they do not need to be sports related but are events or actions that you have seen as failings. Below that, write down the positives about the 'mistake'.

Success comes…when you automatically regard an error as a chance to improve next time.

Date: 22/04/2025

Negative Event 1: I lost a point by missing my backhand.

Positive Spin 1: I did well to get into position where I could at least get my hand on that chance. Next time I will catch it.

Negative Event 2:

Positive Spin 2:

Date:

Negative Event 1:

Positive Spin 1:

Negative Event 2:

Positive Spin 2:

Drill 42: Sandwich Assessment

It is human nature to focus on the negatives of our own performance. Top athletes do not do this. They see failings as opportunities to improve and are conscious of their successes.

The Drill: At the end of any sports session do a short self-evaluation. Start with a success and end with a success. In between the sandwich of success put a filling of an area to improve. Consider something that did not work and determine how you can improve this area.

Success comes…when your self-evaluation leaves you feeling positive about your performance.

Success 1 (at start of session):

Area to Improve 1:

Area to Improve 2:

Area to Improve 3:

Success 2 (at end of session):

Drill 43: Null the Error

The Drill: Encourage a teammate when they make an error. Do this (to different team mates ideally) at least five times during the session.

Success comes…when we automatically find ourselves being positive towards our teammates, even when they make a mistake. In turn, of course, we have turned ourselves into a positive influence and demonstrated leadership. How good will that make us feel about ourselves?

Drill 44: Get a New Frame for the Photo…

Another drill which utilizes the value of your notebook.

The Drill: Get two different colored pens, a red one for the negative thought and a green one for the new frame for the thought. At the end of each day, spend two minutes writing down a negative thought you have had. Write it in red and draw a wiggly frame around it. Then turn the thought into a positive one, using your green pen, and draw a strong, straight frame around it. For example, I dropped a catch (red). I made the best effort I could to reach that catch. I'll get it next time (green).

Negative Thought 1:	Reframed Negative Thought 1:
I dropped a catch.	I made the best effort I could to get that catch. I'll get it next time.
Negative Thought 2:	Reframed Negative Thought 2:
Negative Thought 3:	Reframed Negative Thought 3:

Success comes…when you automatically see positives even in disappointments.

Cool Under Fire: Eric Dier's Playbook for Keeping Your Head When the Heat's On

Emotional Regulation – The Ability to Maintain Focus in High Pressure Situations

Soccer fans will most probably have heard of Eric Dier. England and Tottenham Hotspurs supporters will know him reasonably well, as might those who follow Bayern Munich. But for most readers, the name will elicit a quick search of the memory, a shake of the head and a decision to move on. Yet his story is worth telling, and illustrates another kind of mental strength.

Eric Dier achieved something that a mixture of circumstances, technique and astonishing focus under the greatest of pressures imaginable – in fact, for most of us, not imaginable. It marks him down forever in the history of English sporting achievements.

For the story to make sense something must be understood about the English passion for soccer – football as it is called exclusively in the country (we'll stick with 'soccer' for now...) England sees itself as the home of soccer. It claims the birthright to the sport. Tellingly, perhaps, this is most likely an inaccurate claim. The sport most probably originated in China in the second century BC. The average English soccer fan likes to boast that the game belongs to the people. That it is the property of the working classes. Again, pretty much untrue. The modern game did originate in Victorian England, but in the public (by which, in that curious way of the English, we mean private) schools. It did not originate among the terraced streets of northern towns during the industrial revolution.

Since this is a book about mental strength, it is perhaps worth noting that this denial of truths is a kind of mental weakness, a sort of delusion on the part of many English soccer fans about the state of their game. Read English newspapers in the build up to a world cup or European championship and they will follow the same line. Total conviction that not only will England win the tournament, but that it is their right to win the tournament. Followed by hyperbolic criticism of everybody associated with the team and then, when the inevitable happens, a ferocious call for the sacking of the manager. Even Gareth Southgate, England's previous manager at the time of writing, suffered this fate. Despite the fact that Southgate is a deeply honorable, honest, open, forward thinking, man who communicated freely with the press, and even more importantly changed both the culture and the success of the England team.

Of course, for one fleeting moment, in 1966, England were the best soccer team on the planet, defeating their nemesis Germany (West Germany as it was in those days) in the final of the World Cup. Joint favorites going into the next tournament disappointment followed as the Germans got their revenge in the quarters. England took it hard. They didn't qualify again in the 1970s. A semi-final in 1990 apart (more on which shortly) followed four decades of underachievement and disappointment. A couple of quarter finals, but generally once the group stage passes, England lose and go home. A big reason being their abject failure at penalty shoot outs. It becomes an English disease, a psychological burden on the team. Coaches tried practicing, not practicing (astonishing, that one), players who missed, including Southgate in his playing days, were firstly vilified and then paid thousands to make consciously ironic TV commercials. Consider this record in major tournaments:

- 1990 – lost 4-3 to West Germany in the world cup.
- 1996 – won 4-2 over Spain in the European championships.
- 1996 – lost 6-5 to Germany in the next round of the competition.
- 1998 – lost 4-3 to Belgium in a pre-world cup competition.
- 1998 – lost 6-5 to Argentina in the world cup.
- 2004 – lost 6-5 to Portugal in the European championships.
- 2006 – lost 3-1 to the same team in the world cup.

- 2012 – lost 4-2 to Italy in the European championships.

Which brings us to Eric Dier. Dier is a fine footballer, one who represented his country and enjoyed a strong career in the Premier League. But, to be fair, whilst the other sports players in this book are not only elite players, but world class performers who, for a while at least, were among the best two or three in the world in their sport, often the very best, not even Eric Dier's parents would claim their son quite achieved those heights. He is an elite athlete, a top performer, but not of the class of others of his era, such as Lionel Messi or Cristiano Ronaldo.

But when England draw with Columbia in the first knock out round of the 2018 World Cup and the referee signals for penalties, collectively English soccer fans shake their heads and prepare for the worst. England cannot do penalty shoot outs. They do not have the focus, the mental strength, to come through them.

But the new manager, Gareth Southgate, has instilled something into a group of journeymen international footballers lit only by the odd spark of genuine class. Harry Kane, the star man, scores. Marcus Rashford, a speedy wide player nets. Then Jordan Henderson, Mr. Midfield Reliability, has his penalty saved. 'Here we go...' breathes the nation. Incredibly, though Mateus Uribe goes for power and hits the crossbar. Kieran Trippier, strong on the dead ball, scores and Columbia misses.

One penalty to win. 'It can't happen,' says England. 'It won't happen...' Who can imagine the weight on Dier's shoulders, the pressure on him, the distraction. But he remains focused, concentrates; he steps up, strikes the ball firmly, and although the keeper gets a hand to it, the ball enters the net.

Can we begin to imagine the distractions pressing in on Eric Dier's mind as he makes the long walk from the halfway line to the penalty spot? Distractions from the crowd, the boos of opposing fans and the cheers of your own. Distraction from the keeper, doing everything he can to gain his own mental edge. But mostly, the distraction of the weight of history.

Mental strength. Focus under pressure. England will go on to win two of their next three penalty shootouts. The disease is cured.

Whether Eric Dier's inspirational penalty inspires you depends very much on whether you're an England football fan, We can all learn the important mental strength principle of maintaining calm under intense pressure, which is a byproduct of emotional regulation. We can work on this with some of the drills below.

Drill 45: Pre-Match Regulation

Work out what works best for you in terms of pre-match relaxation. Try having a warm bath or shower, listening to music (and what kind of music – Ian Wright, a former striker for England and Arsenal is a big hip-hop fan, but would begin his pre-match calming routine by listening to classical music!), doing stretches, just sitting quietly, reading…

Success comes…we are all different so it may take us a while to find what works for us, but then we use it as a key part of our pre-match routine to keep us stress controlled during our game or competition.

Drill 46: Rhythmic Walking

Another meditation style exercise which again focuses on breathing.

The Drill: Stand and move your foot up and down. As you bring your foot down breathe in and breathe out as you lift your foot up.

Success comes…when you feel the rhythm of your movement fit into the rhythm of your breathing. (It is incredibly relaxing and mind clearing!)

Drill 47: Mantras: Getting in the Now

Time for some drills which focus on the importance of a mantra. Our first drill helps us to think in the present. It is natural to either look forward to an event, a match, or an event likely to occur in the match. It is equally a part of human nature to reflect back, either to dwell in past glories or, more often, to kick ourselves for making a mistake. But, although the following is a cliché, it is a good one: *we are as good as our current performance.*

The Drill: Write down three statements in the past tense, e.g. 'I was happy yesterday' and three in the future. For example, I will be going out to eat tomorrow.' The content of the statements doesn't matter. Say each statement in your head three times. But in the present tense. For example, 'I am happy' or 'I am going out to eat'. You can do it in the space below or in your notebook.

Success comes…when we can automatically put ourselves in the now when we choose to.

Past Statements:

Statement 1: _____

Statement 2: _____

Statement 3: _____

Future Statements:

Statement 1: _____

Statement 2: _____

Statement 3: _____

Make Each Statement Present:

Statement 1: _____

Statement 2: _____

Statement 3: _____

Drill 48: Mantras: Getting in the Now: Grounding Through the Senses:

We can train ourselves to use our senses to bring us into the now, and to help us relax. This drill is ideal for pre-match/competition focus. It is a little long to use in-competition.

The Drill: Using the environment we are in, find five items you can see, four you can hear, three you can touch, two you can smell and one you can taste. Do not rush this, and you can take 2 minutes to complete each item with a total of 10 minutes.

Success comes…when we begin to relax during the first 'sense' phase of the drill.

Drill 49: Boxed Breathing

This is a well-known technique useful for high pressure situations, and for those in the early stages of developing their mental strength.

The Drill: Breath in – count to four slowly as you breathe in. 'One Mississippi, two Mississippi…' etc. Hold the breath for another count of four. Breathe out for another count of four. Repeat twice.

Success comes…when the relaxation and focus comes on the first cycle of the drill.

Drill 50: Controlling those Emotions

Passion is brilliant in sport, essential to be at your best. Until it gets out of control. This won't be a problem for everyone, but if you know that…

You get over excited.

You lose perspective.

You get angry with teammates, the opposition or the referee.

You lose your cool…

Then controlling that excess emotion is essential to improve your performance. After all, getting disqualified or sent off is the worst thing you can do both to yourself and your team. The best way to control an emotion is to gain a distance from it.

The Drill: In sport and everyday life, when you feel a strong emotion, stop (perhaps use one of the 'locks' identified in other drills to achieve) and tell yourself what emotion you are experiencing. The key here is to tell yourself in the third person. So, 'This emotion is anger' rather than 'I am angry.'

Success comes…when you can identify and keep distance from your extreme emotions.

Drill 51: Random Meditation

This meditation drill is handy for people who struggle to focus for any period on a particular object or activity. For example, people who suffer from attention deficit disorders.

The Drill: Find a quiet spot and spend five minutes on the exercise. Observe as much as you can. As you spot something ask yourself a question: Why do I like that? Or 'How does that happen?' Open questions, and non-judgmental ones.

Success comes…when your curiosity is stimulated. Now you are more aware of your surroundings, and better able to act in unison with them.

Reward 3:

As a reward for completing this chapter, I'd like to offer you my free book on "Soccer Mental Toughness". It's a book on skills, strategies and exercises to use your mind to improve performances on the field. Just scan the QR code to get your book.

30 Days to a Titanium Mind: Your Mental Toughness Bootcamp

30 Day Mental Exercise Plan

Because improving our mental strength is best achieved through a holistic approach, many of these drills will help to impact several aspects of mental fortitude. In other words, the drills will help generally with the growth of our mental strength. But also, we will see this aspect of our athletic performance improve as a whole, rather than element by element.

As we saw with the elite athletes used as examples in the previous chapters, their mental strength was across the board, even though we focused on one element per chapter.

A thirty-day plan is a good way to begin our process towards strengthening the way our mind supports our performance. Really, though, this is an on-going process throughout our sporting careers. It is human nature to have ups and downs in all aspects of our lives. Especially sporting ones. It is the nature of sport that sometimes we win, sometimes we do not. Sometimes our own performance is strong, irrespective of the result, sometimes less so. Every sports player feels low after a poor performance, or a defeat. The strongest, though, are quickly able to turn negatives into learning and improvement opportunities, They pass through their disappointment rapidly and move on to the next stages – recovery and enhancement.

Drills such as the ones which follow need to be learned, practiced and employed. We can then use them to move even more quickly beyond disappointment, doubt, lack of self-confidence and their accompanying (and most dangerous) partner... lack of self-esteem.

Each of the drills ends with a list of the chapters to which it best relates. As you prepare your personal program, the following list of suggestions will help to make it successful.

1) Aim to work on three drills per day.
2) Spend no longer than ten minutes on each drill. Little and often is better than long periods of mental training.
3) Try to spread the drills throughout the day rather than doing all three at the same point of the day.

Every athlete is unique, so every plan will be individual to your own needs. **Mindfulness** drills are particularly effective at the beginning of a day, so these are good ones to use first thing in the morning. **Breathing** and **Focus** type drills are good for bringing calm, so are useful to fit in during your day. Perhaps at a lunch time, or when you get home from work, school or college. **Notebook** style drills are especially effective towards the end of the day, providing closure on the day's events. You have written down what you want to say, and can now close the book on your sporting mental training. Until tomorrow at least.

Organizing Your Personal Schedule:

- Stick to the 3 short activities per day routine. You don't want it to become a drag.
- Use the examples in the book to decide which area of mental strength you wish to work on first. This probably should be an area in which you are already middling. Don't start with your biggest challenge, as this will be the area which takes most work and will therefore take the longest to master.

Finally, below is a sample 30-day program. Of course, even better is to design your own table to record the information, which is important to you, or record the drills in your journal/notebook. Do note, though, how the drills are repeated until they are mastered and begin to have an impact. Repetition also helps us to call on them at other times, such as during a competition or when our confidence might be low.

For the last 2 days, you pick the 6 drills that positively impacted you the most and write them down and complete them.

Week 1: Build Resilience and Focus

Day 1:

Morning Drill: Mantra: Be Positive (1)

Afternoon Drill: In The Now

Evening Drill: Visualize Historic Comebacks

Day 2:

Morning Drill: Mantra: Be Positive (2)

Afternoon Drill: Walking for Strength

Evening Drill: How to Reverse Losses

Day 3:

Morning Drill: Mantra: Be Positive (3)

Afternoon Drill: Dress Rehearsal

Evening Drill: Have a Realistic Measure for Success

Day 4:

Morning Drill: Mantra: Be Positive (4)

Afternoon Drill: The Mental MRI – 'M' for Meditate

Evening Drill: Rhythmic Walking

Day 5:

Morning Drill: Breathe for Brilliance

Afternoon Drill: The Mental MRI – 'R' for Reflect

Evening Drill: Rhythmic Walking

Day 6:

Morning Drill: Breathe for Brilliance

Afternoon Drill: The Mental MRI – 'I' for Initiate

Evening Drill: The Dress Rehearsal

Day 7:

Morning Drill: Mantra: Be Positive (4)

Afternoon Drill: In The Now

Evening Drill: Visualize Historic Comebacks

Week 2: Enhance Self-Discipline and Build Confidence

Day 1:

Morning Drill: The Cold Start Drill

Afternoon Drill: Mindfulness with Nutrition

Evening Drill: Know Yourself

Day 2:

Morning Drill: The Cold Start Drill

Afternoon Drill:

Evening Drill: Be Your Favorite Mentor

Day 3:

Morning Drill: Distraction Kill Drill

Afternoon Drill: Mindfulness with Nutrition

Evening Drill: Daily Micro-Wins Log

Day 4:

Morning Drill: Distraction Kill Drill

Afternoon Drill: Mindfulness with Nutrition

Evening Drill: Daily Micro-Wins Log

Day 5:

Morning Drill: Win the First Hour Drill

Afternoon Drill: Mindfulness with Nutrition

Evening Drill: Daily Micro-Wins Log

Day 6:

Morning Drill: Win the First Hour Drill

Afternoon Drill: Pressure Simulation Drill

Evening Drill: Daily Micro-Wins Log

Day 7:

Morning Drill: In-competition sensory support

Afternoon Drill: Pressure Simulation Drill

Evening Drill: Self Evaluate Our Strategy

Week 3: Mental Flexibility with Intrinsic Motivation

Day 1:

Morning Drill: In-competition sensory support

Afternoon Drill: Get Advice on the Strategy

Evening Drill: T is for Timed Limit on Goals

Day 2:

Morning Drill: Mantras: Getting in the Now

Afternoon Drill: Get Advice on the Strategy

Evening Drill: Personal Goal

Day 3:

Morning Drill: Mantras: Getting in the Now: Grounding In the Senses

Afternoon Drill: Get Advice on the Strategy

Evening Drill: The "Why 5x" Drill

Day 4:

Morning Drill: The Eton Fives Conundrum

Afternoon Drill: Random Meditation

Evening Drill: Personal Goal 2 (Set your 2nd Personal Goal)

Day 5:

Morning Drill: The Eton Fives Conundrum

Afternoon Drill: Random Meditation

Evening Drill: The "Why 5x" Drill

Day 6:

Morning Drill: Keep Perspective in what you do

Afternoon Drill: Random Meditation

Evening Drill: Don't Neglect Your Studies

Day 7:

Morning Drill: Keep Perspective in what you do

Afternoon Drill: Random Meditation

Evening Drill: Don't Neglect Your Studies

Week 4: Power Optimism with Emotional Regulation

Day 1:

Morning Drill: Pre-Match Regulation

Afternoon Drill: Boxed Breathing

Evening Drill: Retaking the Picture

Day 2:

Morning Drill: Boxed Breathing

Afternoon Drill: Rhythmic Walking

Evening Drill: Sandwich Assessment

Day 3:

Morning Drill: Controlling those Emotions

Afternoon Drill: Boxed Breathing

Evening Drill: Null the Error

Day 4:

Morning Drill: Random Meditation

Afternoon Drill: Sandwich Assessment

Evening Drill: Get a New Frame for the Photo

Day 5:

Morning Drill: Mantras: Getting In the Now

Afternoon Drill: Null the Error

Evening Drill: Retaking the Picture

Day 6:

Morning Drill: Mantras: Getting In the Now: Grounding In the Senses

Afternoon Drill: Sandwich Assessment

Evening Drill: Retaking the Picture

Day 7:

Morning Drill: Mantras: Getting In the Now: Grounding In the Senses

Afternoon Drill: Null the Error

Evening Drill: Sandwich Assessment

For the last 2 days, pick the 6 drills that had the biggest positive impact on you and write them down below.

Day 29:

Morning Drill: _____

Afternoon Drill: _____

Evening Drill: _____

Day 30:

Morning Drill: _____

Afternoon Drill: _____

Evening Drill: _____

The end... almost!

Reviews are not easy to come by.

As an independent author with a tiny marketing budget, I rely on readers, like you, to leave a short review on Amazon.

Even if it's just a sentence or two!

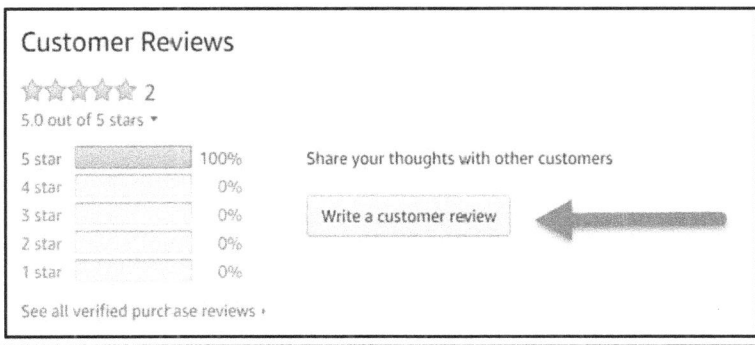

So if you enjoyed the book, please...

Thank you from the bottom of my heart for purchasing this book and reading it to the end.

Other Books We Recommend

If you liked this book, you will also like the books below:

Mental Toughness for Young Athletes (Parent's Guide) by Troy Horne

Young Athletes Ultimate Guide to Mental Toughness by Chad Metcalf

The Mamba Mentality by Kobe Bryant

If you're interested in soccer training and soccer coaching books, you can check out other books by Chest Dugger below..

https://www.amazon.com/stores/Chest-Dugger/author/B0BWSKLCNX

And you can check out our Soccer Coaching blog below:

https://abiprod.com

www.ingramcontent.com/pod-product-compliance
Lightning Source LLC
Chambersburg PA
CBHW061208070526
4483CB00025B/3164